J
BIO
CISNEROS

Krohn, Katherine E.

Evelyn Cisneros: prima ballerina

Biographies

Evelyn Cisneros
Prima Ballerina

by Katherine Krohn

Capstone press®

Mankato, Minnesota

Fact Finders is published by Capstone Press,
151 Good Counsel Drive, P.O. Box 669, Mankato, Minnesota 56002.
www.capstonepress.com

Library of Congress Cataloging-in-Publication Data
Krohn, Katherine E.
    Evelyn Cisneros : prima ballerina / by Katherine Krohn.
    p. cm. — (Fact finders. Biographies. Great Hispanics)
    Includes bibliographical references and index.
    ISBN-13: 978-0-7368-6416-9 (hardcover)
    ISBN-10: 0-7368-6416-4 (hardcover)
    1. Cisneros, Evelyn, 1958– —Juvenile literature. 2. Ballet dancers—United States—
Biography—Juvenile literature. 3. Ballerinas—United States—Biography—Juvenile
literature. I. Title. II. Series.
GV1785.C57K76 2007
792.8092—dc22   2005037984

Summary: An introduction to the life of Evelyn Cisneros, the Mexican American dancer
    who became the prima ballerina with the San Francisco Ballet.

Editorial Credits
John Bliss and Jennifer Murtoff (Navta Associates), editors; Juliette Peters, set designer;
    Jan Calek (Navta Associates), book designer; Wanda Winch, photo researcher/
    photo editor

Photo Credits
Courtesy Ronald Reagan Library, 5 (both); Huntington Beach Conference and Visitors Bureau,
Huntington Beach, California, 9; Image courtesy of Evelyn Cisneros, 7, 8, 13, 14, 22 (right), 23 (top),
26; Lloyd Englert, cover; San Francisco Chronicle/Brant Ward, 23 (bottom); San Francisco Chronicle/
Deanne Fitzmaurice, 1; San Francisco Chronicle/Robin Weiner, 25; San Francisco Performing Arts
Library & Museum, 15, 17, 21, 22 (left); San Francisco Performing Arts Library & Museum/Arne
Folkedal, 18, 19; San Francisco Performing Arts Library & Museum/Bill Acheson, 27; San Francisco
Performing Arts Library & Museum/Marty Sohl, 11

A special thank-you goes to Evelyn Cisneros, who graciously devoted her time and energy
    to make this volume possible.

Table of Contents

Chapter 1

Dancing on Air

Evelyn Cisneros danced joyfully across the stage. She gracefully moved her body to the music. To Cisneros, dancing was as natural as speaking.

Cisneros was a ballerina with the famous San Francisco Ballet. On this day in 1982, she and other dancers had been invited to the White House. The program was shown live on television. From the front row, President Ronald Reagan and his wife watched the performance.

Afterward, Cisneros and the other dancers posed for a photo with the Reagans. They complimented her performance. Cisneros was proud. She had worked very hard to get to this moment.

In 1982, Cisneros performed at the White House for President and Mrs. Reagan (left). After the performance, the dancers posed with the Reagans (top). Cisneros is on the left in the front row.

Chapter 2

Shy Girl

On November 18, 1958, Fred and Esther Cisneros welcomed a baby girl into the world. Fred and Esther named their new daughter Evelyn. Two years later, after their son Robert was born, the family moved to Huntington Beach, California.

All kinds of music, including classical, jazz, and gospel, filled the Cisneros home. Fred Cisneros played the clarinet. Esther Cisneros played the violin. They taught their daughter to enjoy music.

When she was four, Cisneros played an angel in a Christmas program. Even though she was with other children, Cisneros felt shy and embarrassed about being in front of the audience.

Fred and Esther Cisneros helped their daughter develop an interest in music and dance.

As Cisneros sang, she slowly lifted her costume over her head. Cisneros thought that if she couldn't see the people watching, they couldn't see her.

▲ Cisneros (back row, second from left) poses with family members at her grandfather's retirement party.

Happy Family

Cisneros was part of a big, happy Mexican American family. Each Sunday, Cisneros and her family attended church. The service was in Spanish. After church, the family would eat dinner at one of her grandparents' homes. Cisneros loved the traditional Mexican food her grandmothers cooked.

Cisneros enjoyed seeing her grandparents, aunts, and uncles. She liked to play with her many cousins. Still, Cisneros was very shy. Speaking to anyone outside the family was hard for her.

Cisneros' mother had an idea. She knew her daughter loved music. Cisneros liked to dance to the lively Mexican **mariachi** music at family gatherings. Maybe a dance class would boost seven-year-old Cisneros' confidence.

Cisneros grew up in Huntington Beach, California, a town on the Pacific Ocean ◄ near Los Angeles.

Chapter 3

The Language of Dance

Cisneros liked her new **leotard,** tights, and ballet slippers. But she didn't like ballet class. Cisneros felt nervous dancing in front of people. She worried that she wouldn't be able to do the dance steps.

To avoid going to the class, Cisneros pretended to have stomachaches and headaches. Her mother insisted that she stay in ballet class for one year. At that point, if Cisneros still didn't like ballet, her mother said that she could quit.

Slowly, Cisneros began to enjoy the class. For her, ballet was a new language. Her mother helped her learn that she could "speak" through dance.

Cisneros, shown here dancing *Swan Lake* in 1988, enjoyed ballet because she could speak with her body through dance.

A Real Ballerina

When Cisneros was eight, she started classes with a new dance teacher, Phyllis Cyr. Cyr saw something great in Cisneros. She saw how naturally Cisneros moved to the music. Cisneros had strength, flexibility, and control. Cyr was certain that Cisneros had what it took to become a great ballerina.

QUOTE

"She was the one who really instilled in me a love of dance. I consider her my first real teacher."

—Evelyn Cisneros, speaking about Phyllis Cyr

Sacrifices

When Cisneros was 13, she faced a tough choice. If she wanted to be a professional dancer, she had to start right away. She would have to give all her free time to lessons and rehearsals. Cisneros wouldn't have much time to spend with her family and friends. She would have to quit the track and volleyball teams at school. Cisneros talked it over with her parents. She decided that she wanted a career as a ballet dancer.

◄ By age 13, Cisneros already knew she wanted to be a professional dancer. This photo was taken at the Phyllis Cyr Dance Academy.

Busy Girl

Cisneros became very busy. She ate her lunch in class. That way, Cisneros could leave school early and go to advanced dance classes. After dinner, she drove with other dancers to the Pacific Ballet Theater in Los Angeles. She took more classes there. Cisneros did homework in the car.

Cisneros practices for a production of *Snow White* at the Phyllis Cyr Dance Academy. ⬇

Fitting In

Cisneros was the only Mexican American girl in her ballet class. Her skin was darker than everyone else's. Sometimes she worried that she might not fit in as a ballet dancer.

Cisneros admired **prima ballerina** Maria Tallchief. Tallchief, a Native American, had danced with the New York City Ballet for almost 20 years. She was proof that a person of color could be a professional ballerina.

As a person of color, Maria Tallchief was an inspiration to Cisneros. ➡

Chapter 4

The Big Time

In 1974, Cisneros tried out to take a class at the School of American Ballet. She was thrilled when she was awarded the opportunity. In July, Cisneros boarded a plane to New York City. Cisneros was excited about the class. But the experience was disappointing for her. The ballet directors placed Cisneros in a class that was below her level. Her classmates weren't very nice to her. Cisneros called her parents. She wanted to go home.

Cisneros' parents contacted the San Francisco Ballet School. They told the ballet director about Cisneros and her experience in New York. The director gave Cisneros a scholarship for their summer course.

Cisneros went to the San Francisco Ballet School after leaving the School of American Ballet in New York.

QUOTE

"There's a part inside me that has to do it, to dance, and express myself through movement. I feel that it's a gift, and I feel that to not express that gift would be disregarding it, throwing it away."

—Evelyn Cisneros

Cisneros completed the summer course and was invited to stay for the winter course. Cisneros liked the school. Her love for ballet returned.

Ups and Downs

In 1976, Cisneros started an internship with the San Francisco Ballet. Two days after her arrival, Cisneros was put to the test. A dancer was not able to perform. Cisneros would need to fill her place for a performance that evening. Cisneros had only five hours to learn a long part of the ballet. That evening, Cisneros performed in front of a packed audience. She felt proud. She had shown that she was a fast learner and a talented dancer.

▲ Cisneros dances a summer school demonstration in 1976 with San Francisco Ballet member Don Schwennessen.

QUOTE

"My mother, father, and brother would drive up at least once a month to see me, and I would go down when my ballet schedule allowed."
—Evelyn Cisneros

One day, Cisneros waited backstage to perform. She wore tights and a **tutu,** just like the other dancers. Her hair was in a bun, the same as everyone else.

The **ballet master** said she didn't look like the other ballerinas. He thought her skin was too dark. He told her to put on light body makeup. Cisneros felt humiliated. But if she wanted to keep her job, she had to do as he said.

During 1976, Cisneros proved her skill. She became a member of the San Francisco Ballet in 1977. ⬇

Prima Ballerina

Cisneros did her job well. In 1977, she joined the San Francisco Ballet as a member. In 1979, artistic director Michael Smuin created Cisneros' first solo role. It was a ballet about Native Americans called *Song for a Dead Warrior.* Cisneros performed her role perfectly. The audience gave the performers a standing ovation. Cisneros was presented with a bouquet of lavender roses. She thought, "Oh, my gosh! *This is it!*"

Choreographers enjoyed creating roles for Cisneros. She became known as a prima ballerina. Still, she practiced the same moves she did as a girl. She never stopped striving for perfection.

Cisneros' first starring role with the San Francisco Ballet was *Song for a Dead Warrior* in 1979.

In 1980, Cisneros danced in *The Tempest* with Tomm Rudd.

Cisneros traveled with an exhibition to Monterrey, Mexico.

Starring Roles

Cisneros' work paid off. Over the next several years, she starred in many classical ballet roles. In 1980, Cisneros played Miranda in *The Tempest*. She also played lead roles in *Sleeping Beauty*, *Swan Lake*, *The Nutcracker*, *Cinderella*, and *Romeo and Juliet*.

Love at Last

Cisneros was at the height of her career. In 1996, after two previous marriages, Cisneros married Stephen Legate. He was handsome, kind, and a brilliant dancer. Cisneros knew their partnership would last a lifetime.

▲ Cisneros and Legate danced *Aquilarco* together in 1999.

Chapter 6

Moving On

In 1999, Cisneros made a big decision. After 23 years, she retired from the San Francisco Ballet. On May 9, 1999, the ballet company honored Cisneros. At the event, Cisneros, Legate, and other dancers performed.

The mayor of San Francisco declared the week Cisneros retired as "Evelyn Cisneros Week." In March 2000, a television station aired a documentary about Cisneros' life—*Evelyn Cisneros, Moving On*.

After retirement, Cisneros wanted to focus on family. In 2000, Cisneros and Legate adopted a baby boy, Ethan. They adopted a second child, Sophia, in 2005.

Cisneros receives a standing ovation after her final performance, *Sleeping Beauty*.

▲ Cisneros, with son Ethan, teaches a ballet education class in San Francisco.

QUOTE

"Life is really only a series of new beginnings, and just when you feel at the top of your world, that world seems to rotate and you find yourself at the beginning once again."
—Evelyn Cisneros

Life After Dancing

Today, Cisneros works part time as the Ballet Education Coordinator at the San Francisco Ballet Center for Dance Education. As a part of her job, she speaks and teaches at schools and colleges. She encourages young people to follow their dreams.

Cisneros treasures her memories of ballet dancing. Her heart warms at the thought of her fans or the thrill of an opening night. She's proud of the many leading roles she has played. But her all-time favorite role is her current one. Being a mom is the best job she's ever had.

Fast Facts

Full name: Evelyn Deanne Cisneros-Legate

Birth: November 18, 1958

Parents: Fred Robert Cisneros and Esther Cisneros

Brother: Robert

Hometown: Huntington Beach, California

Husbands: David McNaughton (1978–1979), Robert Sund (1985–1991), Stephen Legate (1996–present)

Children: Ethan and Sophia

Major Roles:
  Princess Aurora in *Sleeping Beauty*
  Odette/Odile in *Swan Lake*
  The Sugar Plum Fairy in
      The Nutcracker
  Cinderella in *Cinderella*
  Juliet in *Romeo and Juliet*
  Principal ballerina in
      Theme and Variations
  Principal role in *Lambarena*
  Lise in *La Fille mal Gardée*

Time Line

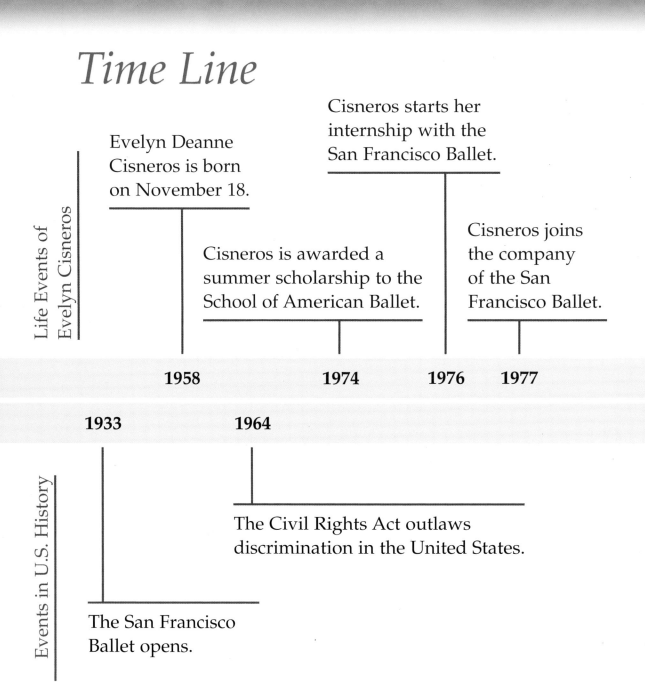

Life Events of Evelyn Cisneros

Evelyn Deanne Cisneros is born on November 18.

Cisneros starts her internship with the San Francisco Ballet.

Cisneros is awarded a summer scholarship to the School of American Ballet.

Cisneros joins the company of the San Francisco Ballet.

1958   1974   1976   1977

1933   1964

Events in U.S. History

The Civil Rights Act outlaws discrimination in the United States.

The San Francisco Ballet opens.

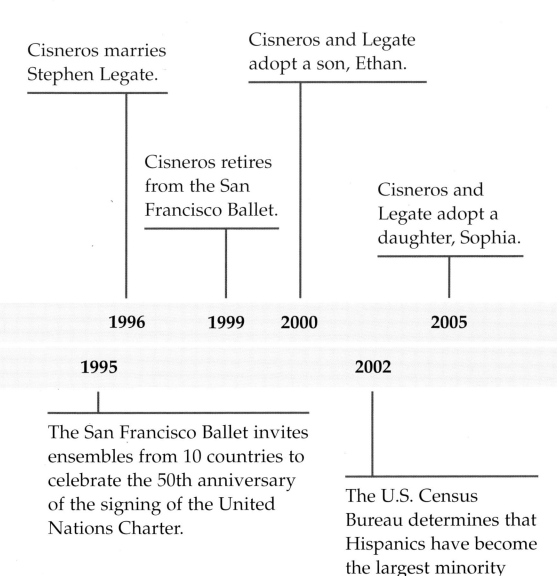

Cisneros marries Stephen Legate.

Cisneros and Legate adopt a son, Ethan.

Cisneros retires from the San Francisco Ballet.

Cisneros and Legate adopt a daughter, Sophia.

1996   1999   2000   2005

1995   2002

The San Francisco Ballet invites ensembles from 10 countries to celebrate the 50th anniversary of the signing of the United Nations Charter.

The U.S. Census Bureau determines that Hispanics have become the largest minority in the United States.

Glossary

ballet master (bal-LAY MASS-tur)—the person who directs, teaches, and rehearses dancers for a ballet company

choreographer (kor-ee-OG-ruh-fur)—someone who arranges dance steps for a ballet or show

leotard (LEE-uh-tard)—a snug, one-piece garment worn by dancers

mariachi (mah-ree-AH-chee)—a Mexican street band

prima ballerina (PREE-muh bal-uh-REE-nuh)—the main female dancer in a ballet company

tutu (TOO-too)—a short ballet skirt made of several layers of stiff net

Internet Sites

FactHound offers a safe, fun way to find Internet sites related to this book. All of the sites on FactHound have been researched by our staff.

Here's how:

1. Visit *www.facthound.com*

2. Choose your grade level.

3. Type in this book ID **0736864164** for age-appropriate sites. You may also browse subjects by clicking on letters, or by clicking on pictures and words.

4. Click on the **Fetch It** button.

FactHound will fetch the best sites for you!

Read More

Grover, Lorie Ann. *On Pointe.* New York: Margaret K. McElderry Books, 2004.

Speck, Scott, and Evelyn Cisneros. *Ballet for Dummies.* For Dummies. Hoboken, N.J.: Wiley, 2003.

Yolen, Jane, and Heidi E. Y. Stemple. *The Barefoot Book of Ballet Stories.* Cambridge, Mass.: Barefoot Books, 2004.

Index